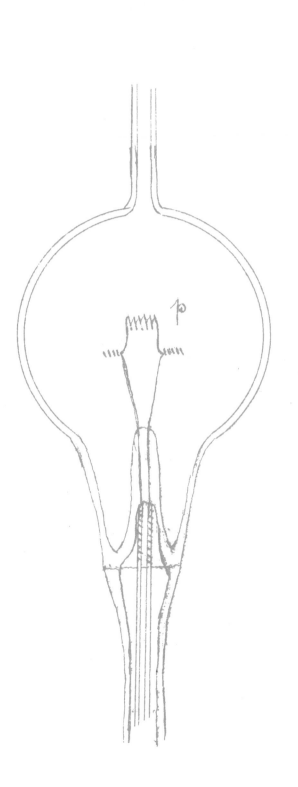

THE LIGHTBULB

THE LIGHTBULB

JOSEPH WALLACE
Foldout illustration by Toby Welles

Atheneum Books for Young Readers

Atheneum Books for Young Readers
An imprint of Simon & Schuster
Children's Publishing Division
1230 Avenue of the Americas
New York, New York 10020

FIRST
EDITION

Produced by
CommonPlace Publishing
2 Morse Court
New Canaan, Connecticut 06840

Art Director: Samuel N. Antupit
Editor: Sharon AvRutick
Picture Research: Jean Martin
Production Design: Cheung/Crowell Design

Printed in Hong Kong through Global Interprint

10 9 8 7 6 5 4 3 2 1

ISBN 0-689-82816-0

Library of Congress
Card Catalog Number: 98-89824

For Karla Olson, with gratitude and fond memories of dinosaurs and the deep blue sea

Page 1
Thomas Alva Edison, the inventor of the lightbulb, was also responsible for a number of
other inventions, including the phonograph and the movie camera.

Pages 2–3
This illustration shows a variety of glass bulbs right from the mold before being assembled
into lightbulbs.

CONTENTS

1

THE SEARCH FOR LIGHT

What did you do last night? Did you go anywhere by car? Do your homework? Watch a movie?

Without the lightbulb, there would be no cars on the road at night, since it would be too dangerous to drive if there were no headlights and streetlights. There would be no movies — lightbulbs light up not only the theater, but the movie screen itself — and restaurants might have to close at dusk. There would be no shopping malls to visit; no one would build stores indoors, away from the sun, if lightbulbs didn't exist.

A life without lightbulbs is pretty hard to imagine, isn't it? But it shouldn't be, because lightbulbs haven't been around for that long. There are people still alive today who remember the time before lightbulbs came into widespread use. It wasn't until 1879 that a young genius named Thomas Edison invented the first working lightbulb — and changed the world.

Of course, Thomas Edison wasn't the first to try to design a cheap, safe, and bright way of illuminating houses, shops, factories, and dark nights. Almost since the beginnings of human history, people have been searching for better methods of lighting their way.

Undoubtedly, the first light source other than the moon or sun — the first that

Opposite
People have long searched for ways to light the darkness. Candles were only one solution.

7

people could control — was fire. Coming upon a smoldering tree stump set aflame by a lightning strike, some smart early humans must have thought, "We can use that."

And use it they did. Humans were the first inhabitants of earth to harness fire, to use it for warmth and to cook food. At some point they even learned to create it, by whacking two rocks together or rubbing the point of a stick against another piece of wood.

One of the most important uses of fire was for illumination. Carrying a lit torch — a thick piece of wood, with perhaps one end dipped into animal grease, or fat — allowed people to move around on moonless nights, while also giving some protection from fierce animals that might be on the lookout for a tasty midnight snack.

Having discovered fire's usefulness as a light source, prehistoric people immediately began to work on improving it. Torches were fine for travel, but what about when you wanted to stop for the night? One early solution was a container — perhaps a hollow stone or a large shell — that held flaming wood or grease. When placed on the ground or atop a nearby rock, the small fire inside the container cast enough light to suddenly make it possible for people to eat, repair their weapons, patch their clothes. At the very dawn of history, humans invented the first lamp.

What was next? Two thousand or more years ago, someone discovered that a piece of string sticking out from a chunk of beeswax — or even from solid fat from meat — would burn slowly and cast a flickering but acceptable light. The candle was born.

Candles, of course, were a big success. They achieved their current form in the seventh century and did the job so well that they were still in widespread use for lighting a century ago. But they were far from perfect. They flickered and burned down quickly and could be dangerous if left unattended. Not only could the flame itself injure people or animals, but it could also set fire to buildings, clothes, or other objects.

Opposite
Early light sources were dangerous — the open flame of this candle might easily set paper or fabric aflame — as well as ineffective. Though it was possible to drink tea by the candle's flickering light, reading or writing for long was almost impossible.

Above
Before the lightbulb, people made do with what they had to light a room. As a young man, Abraham Lincoln not only walked miles to school through the snow each day (as the story goes), but he also did his homework by firelight.

Right
It was possible to have a fancy ball at night in the mid-nineteenth century, but the oil or gas lamps used to light them were expensive, unsafe, and often smoky. Even getting to the ball after sunset was a challenge: "Owing to the difficulty of driving in the dark," wrote one party-goer, "invitations in the country were, when possible, issued for times when the moon shone bright."

Perhaps the worst drawback was that candles didn't do a very good job of lighting a room. A candle in the middle of the dinner table may be pretty, but can you imagine trying to read or write for long by its flickering light?

People continued hunting for other light sources. At one point or another, men and women must have set fire to the oil extracted from every nut, leaves from every plant, and fat from every animal, hoping to find the one substance that would cast the strongest light, burn for the longest possible time with the least smoke, and maybe even smell good to boot.

One substance that did work was whale oil. Whales are covered in blubber — thick layers of fat that help keep them warm in the cold oceans. When boiled in large cauldrons, the blubber produced an oil that made a terrific fuel

Often, as the famous nineteenth-century French painter Claude Monet showed in his painting *Le Diner* ("Dinner"), a single lamp would cast a pool of light where the family was gathered, leaving the rest of the room in darkness.

Manufacturers could make grand promises for oil and gas lamps ("Odorless! Nonflammable!" claims this advertisement), but by 1892, when this French poster appeared, the public was all too aware of the disadvantages of those lighting sources.

for lamps. Whale oil burned so well, in fact, that it opened the door to the first widespread lighting of towns and cities. Whale-oil lamps, which gave off a comparatively strong, steady light, became a common sight on streets and in houses alike in the 1600s and 1700s.

But there was a problem with whale oil — its supply was limited. As the demand for the oil grew, so did the number of whaling ships searching the seas, until the United States and many other countries were sending out hundreds of ships each year. By the mid-1800s, these ships were killing so many whales that the animals' population crashed, and it became almost impossible to find large whales, ones that had enough blubber to produce a lot of oil.

Whale-oil lamps began to stand empty, and people once again had to search for a new fuel for their lamps. They turned to "burning fluid," a mixture of turpentine and alcohol, which was inexpensive and burned with a very bright flame. It provided a fair substitute for whale oil, but also a dangerous one, since the burning fluid itself caught fire so easily that just to light a lamp meant risking an explosion.

The next choice was coal oil, or kerosene, which was a big improvement: It was cheaper and much safer. Still, even when the lamps didn't erupt, tending them was a tedious job. Complained one worker at the American Museum of Natural History in New York City, where the entranceways were lit by kerosene lanterns: "I had to clean, trim, and refill those lamps twice a week after open nights at the Museum — a nasty job during a bitterly cold winter and at the salary of $20 a month."

Another problem was that even the best kerosene lamps could be smoky and might smell bad. If you left one burning long enough, you might find your walls, clothes, and other surfaces covered by a thin layer of greasy oil.

Natural gas was another possibility. Since ancient times, people had known of an invisible gas coming out of the ground or water that could suddenly catch fire. Many ancient cultures considered such fires — and natural gas itself — to be a creation of gods or demons, and they left it alone.

Other cultures, including the ancient Chinese and Greeks, began using natural gas for illumination and during religious ceremonies thousands of years ago. In Europe and the United States, though, no one thought of using this fuel for lighting until much later. It wasn't until 1802, in fact, that an Englishman named William Murdock tried piping natural gas to lanterns hung along the outside of a building. Once the lanterns worked, and nothing exploded, a new generation of lighting had arrived.

By 1820, a resident of Fredonia, New York, was ambitious enough to pipe natural gas to many local houses and stores. Other towns and cities followed Fredonia's example, and soon gaslights could be seen on street corners and in houses across the country.

This was a definite leap forward, but it was far from a perfect solution. Gas lamps didn't smell as bad as kerosene lamps or cover the room in grease, but the slightest puff of air would blow out their flame. Like candles, they frequently set fire to nearby objects if they fell over. Worse, when you tried to blow out the flame of a gas lamp, it might explode instead. People actually died trying to turn out the lights.

None of these light sources made it as easy as it is today for families to read, write, or play games after sunset. And life wasn't much easier outside of the house either. Most stores and businesses had to close as soon as the sun went down. Almost all factories, mills, farms — all the industries that produce the food, clothing, and other products we use every day — operated only during daylight hours. It was simply too dangerous and difficult to try to keep going in darkness or by the weak light sources available.

Except when there was a full moon, wars were fought only during daylight hours; as soon as darkness fell, the battles would come to an end, and everyone would have to wait until sunrise to start again. Even during peacetime, people only risked traveling at night when the moon was bright. If you were going to throw a party after dark, you had to check the phase of the moon in advance, and then hope that the weather stayed clear.

There had to be a better way.

How about electricity? Scientists have known for hundreds of years about the existence of static electricity, the electrical charge produced by friction.

The first serious attempts to harness the power of electricity, however, took place in the middle of the eighteenth century, after the invention in 1745 of the Leyden jar.

The Leyden jar allowed scientists to store static electricity and to release it in a single burst. By producing a strong electrical discharge, scientists at last could begin to study the properties of this powerful force.

For many years, though, experiments with electricity were more like grotesque party tricks. Around 1750, for example, a group of monks formed a line nine hundred feet long. When the monks on the ends of the line touched a group of Leyden jars, a jolt of electricity ran through the entire group, and, in the words of an onlooker, "the whole company at the same instant gave a sudden spring."

Such stunts may have entertained the crowds, but as the years passed more

serious scientists learned an increasing amount about how electricity works. It was only a short step to imagining a world where the bright electrical flash of lightning might be harnessed and used to provide illumination.

But taking the leap from imagining electric light to actually producing it was more difficult than anyone imagined. Even Benjamin Franklin, so famous for flying a kite in a thunderstorm and helping prove that lightning had the same properties as static electricity, gave up, saying that he could find "nothing in the way of use to mankind" from electricity.

Others kept trying, however. In 1802 — forty-five years before Thomas Edison was born — an English chemist named Sir Humphrey Davy heated

Taking care of oil and gas lamps, whether in the home or outside, was a time-consuming and frequently dangerous job. In 1925, American artist Norman Rockwell painted this scene (*opposite*) of a woman polishing, refilling, and trimming the wick of a kerosene lamp. Lighting lamps outdoors (*above*) was "a nasty job during a bitterly cold winter," complained one New York City lamplighter.

Singlephase Mercury Arc Lamp.

Charles P. Steinmetz
Jan. 26th 1903.

A singlephase mercury arc lamp can be operated as follows:

T is a bifurcated tube, with the graphite anodes 1, 2 and the mercury electrodes 3, 4.

C is a small compensator to get the neutral of the A.C. supply. With an A.C. threewire system, as shown dotted, C is unnecessary.

R is the steadying resistance of the arc.

The two forks of the tube then alternate in carrying the two halfwaves as unidirectional current, but both halfwaves combine to a steady current in the steadying arc 3-4. To increase the stability with low voltage, this ionizing arc 3-4 may be shunted with a small storage battery or polarization cells (dry cells) of negligeable capacity, to equalize the current fluctuations by shunting the higher harmonics.

Charles P. Steinmetz

Jan. 26th 1903.

strips of metal by passing an electric current through them. He found that when the strips became hot enough, they would incandesce (glow brightly) for a few seconds before burning up.

The discovery of the principle of incandescence — that running enough electricity through a substance could cause it to glow — was central to Edison's later perfection of the lightbulb. But for Davy, like so many others, the fact that all substances seemed to burn up after just a few seconds of incandescence stopped any further research in its tracks.

But Davy wasn't done laying the groundwork for future improvements in

Before Edison turned his attention to the lightbulb, other inventors came up with the first successful electric light: the arc lamp, a design of which is illustrated *opposite*. An "arc" of electricity leaping between two rods produced a bright but harsh light — suitable for illuminating New York City's Broadway in 1880 (*above*), but not for indoor use.

electric light. In 1809 he took a pair of rods made of charcoal, set their tips a few inches apart, and ran a strong electric current through them. The result: an "arc" of electricity leaped from the tip of one rod to the tip of the other, sending forth a brilliant white light.

Humphrey Davy had invented the arc lamp, the first electric light that could be used to illuminate streets and buildings. The next step was to develop a generator (also called a dynamo) that could send a steady current of electricity through wires to power the arc lamp. By the mid-1800s inventors around the world had designed generators that could serve that purpose.

Arc lamps began to appear on city streets in the 1870s, but for a long time they were looked upon as novelties. "I recall paying a dime in 1877 to view one that was being exhibited at a circus," wrote Francis Jehl, one of Thomas Edison's assistants. In early 1879, only about a dozen buildings in the whole United States were lit by arc lamps.

Soon thereafter, though, the arc lamp began to catch on. In 1880 an American inventor named Charles F. Brush, who had designed one of the first generator-powered arc lamps, was asked to string his lamps along three-quarters of a mile of Broadway in New York City. Before five years had passed, New York alone could boast nearly three thousand of the lamps.

The bright, steady light cast by the arc lamp was by far the most effective source of illumination yet developed, but it wasn't perfect. It was expensive. Worse, the light cast by arc lamps was so bright and harsh that it hurt people's eyes. Since there was no way to control its intensity, the arc lamp was mostly useful for lighting streets, large warehouses, and other open areas. It was, said the great author Robert Louis Stevenson, "a lamp for a nightmare!"

Clearly, the search for an ideal light source would continue. And even as the arc lamp seemed to establish itself as the first choice in New York City and across the world, Thomas Edison went back to an earlier discovery of Humphrey Davy's — the principle of incandescence — in a search for a cheaper, gentler, and long-lasting source of light.

Buy your lamps
where you
see this sign

The initials
of a
friend

What a difference electric light makes
. . . and how much less it costs!

If you lighted your home tonight by oil as you will light it by Edison MAZDA Lamps, the cost would be 20 times as much. Light has become the least expensive of all comforts. It costs less now than before the war. The average family pays less for light than for cream for the breakfast coffee.

So use light freely. A 75-watt Edison MAZDA Lamp gives two and a half times as much light as a 40-watt lamp—but averages only a third of a cent more an hour for current. *And use light right.* Ask an Edison MAZDA Lamp Agent to help you select the *right* types and sizes of lamps for your fixtures. They will increase your comfort immensely —but your electric service bill scarcely at all.

MAZDA—*the mark of a research service*

EDISON MAZDA LAMPS
A GENERAL ELECTRIC PRODUCT

It's a bright idea to use electric light — this was the message in this advertisement for an early Edison lamp.

2

THE LIFE OF A GENIUS

Thomas Edison was born in Milan, Ohio, on February 11, 1847. His parents, Samuel and Nancy Edison, named him Thomas Alva, but from the time of his birth his family and friends called him Alva or even just Al.

Al was a small child, slow to grow and prone to illness. At a time when a chest cold could quickly develop into a fatal infection — antibiotics hadn't been invented yet — his parents often wondered whether their son would survive to become an adult.

Samuel's and Nancy's worries only increased when they saw what sort of boy Al was growing into. Almost from the moment he could walk, he was incredibly curious, willing to try almost anything. In other words, he had the mind of an inventor right from the beginning.

For example, when he was just six years old, he set a fire in his father's barn, just to see what would happen. What happened, of course, was that he burned the barn to the ground. For this "experiment," Al received a beating from his father in the town square — but this punishment, and others to come, didn't put an end to his curiosity.

Like many other people who turn out to be geniuses, Thomas Edison wasn't a very good student. He didn't begin school until he was about eight years old,

Opposite
Thomas Edison wore a piercing gaze and determined expression throughout his extraordinary life.

after his family moved to Port Huron, Michigan, and he found he didn't fit in.

The problem was that his teachers (like almost all teachers of the time) taught by the rote method. Students weren't expected to ask questions, or even think. All they were supposed to do was memorize words, sentences, and math problems, memorize them and repeat them. For someone with the intelligence and creativity of the young Edison, the rote method was torture.

On the other hand, his behavior drove the teachers crazy. One time, he and a classmate lowered a hook and line out of a second-story window, managed to hook a chicken, and pulled it into the classroom. Again, Edison was beaten, and again, the punishment didn't stop him from doing what he pleased.

Edison's problems in school caused his parents and others to wonder whether he'd ever amount to anything. "Some folks thought he was a little addled," his father said. But his mother disagreed, and she decided to take him out of school and teach him at home.

Nancy Edison's decision was probably the best thing that could have happened to young Al, because he was introduced to great literature, world history, and other subjects. Most important of all, he didn't just memorize. His mother allowed him to think for himself.

It was while he was being home-schooled that Edison's parents gave him a science book called *A School Compendium of Natural and Experimental Philosophy*, written by Richard Green Parker. This book contained simple experiments to do at home — and soon Edison had tried them all. He also discovered that inventing was what he wanted to do with his life.

But he would have to wait. His family was in constant money trouble, so by the time he was twelve Edison had left his formal education behind and started to work full-time. His first job was as a "candy butcher" on a train: He sold food and newspapers to passengers on the Grand Trunk Railroad during a four-hour trip between Port Huron and Detroit.

Even as an old man, Edison had fond memories of this job. "The happiest time in my life was when I was twelve years old," he wrote in 1930, when he

When Thomas Alva Edison was a child, his teachers thought him "addled" and predicted that he would never accomplish a thing. But by the time he was twelve, he was already out in the world, working on a train and beginning to conduct the experiments that would be the focus of his life.

was eighty-two. "I was just old enough to have a good time in the world, but not old enough to understand any of its troubles."

The twelve-year-old Edison wasted no time adding to his education. His daily layover in Detroit gave him his first taste of the hustle and bustle of a big city. A world center for the production of chemicals and medicines, Detroit was also a perfect place for Edison to indulge his love of science and experimentation. In fact, with permission of the conductor, he even set up a laboratory in the baggage car of the train — until he accidentally set fire to the train. That put an end to his career as an onboard chemist.

This setback didn't stop Edison from continuing to experiment. "Edison has a wonderfully imaginative mind and also a most remarkable memory," said his friend Henry Ford, one of the first to design a working gasoline-powered car and the founder of the Ford Motor Company. "Yet all of his talents would never have brought anything big into the world had he not had within him that driving force which pushes him on continuously and regardless of everything until he has finished that which he started out to do."

The young Thomas Edison, accidentally setting train cars on fire, may not have known exactly what it was he wanted to do. But he did know he was destined for something more than just a day-to-day job in an office.

In 1863, when he was just sixteen, he took the first in a series of jobs as a telegrapher, sending messages out over electrical lines. These messages, in the form of Morse code (long and short beeps or clicks representing letters of the alphabet), were considered one of technology's greatest leaps at the time.

Experts believed that people would always communicate over long distances with the telegraph, that nothing would ever replace it. "Here, for the first time, the human mind has reached the utmost limit of its progress," wrote an expert in 1882, right around the time the first telephone was being developed.

Edison was a good telegraph operator — fast and accurate at sending out and receiving messages. But the job bored him and, typically, he also couldn't keep from tinkering with chemicals, from seeing what he could invent in his spare time. As a result, he rarely kept a job long. He managed to blow up the telegraph office in Port Huron; he forgot to send out a proper signal, causing a minor train crash in Ontario; and he spilled sulfuric acid that ate through the floor of the office in Louisville, Kentucky. Each of these accidents led to him quickly losing his job.

Battling his boredom, Edison invented several methods of improving communication by telegraph. But his short-sighted supervisors saw only that Edison wasn't paying enough attention to his work and fired him without understanding that his inventions might make their jobs easier.

Taking a job as a telegrapher in Boston, he found that his luck finally began to change. Although he had his usual run-ins with his boss and fellow telegraphers, he loved Boston and found it a city that accepted him and his odd ways, unlike so many other places he'd lived.

While working as a telegrapher for the Western Union Telegraph Company, Edison began to come into contact with other inventors. He'd always believed he could be an inventor himself, and now he was part of a world where people didn't laugh at his dreams. "I have got so much to do, and life is so short," he told a friend there. "I am going to hustle."

And hustle he did. Within three months of arriving in Boston, he had improved an earlier design of his for a duplex telegraph, which allowed two messages to be sent over the same wires at the same time in opposite directions. Though other inventors had already created such a device, Edison's design drew plenty of attention from other telegraphers. In early 1868, just a few months after his arrival in Boston, he and his duplex telegraph were the focus of an article in the *Telegrapher*, an important industry journal.

Encouraged, Edison set up a small workshop with some other hopeful inventors, and in the months that followed he came up with several other inventions. One, a device for electronically counting votes in an election, was a real advance over anything that had come before. The problem was that no politician or government was interested in using it.

From this, the poor young inventor learned an important lesson: Even the most brilliant invention isn't worth much if no one wants to buy it. Edison decided that his future as an inventor would be in designing products that people did want, and that they would pay good money for.

The failure of the vote counter and other inventions, though, brought Edison close to poverty once again. As he had done so often before, he faced his troubles by looking for another place to make his fortune. This time, he chose New York City, where he hoped to raise money for his workshop in Boston.

Edison was so poor by the time he arrived in New York City by steamship that he had to spend his first night sleeping on the city streets. His next step was only a slight improvement: A friend gave him space to sleep and work in the battery room of a telegraph company.

Edison got back to work, but things didn't begin to improve immediately. Back in Boston, his early inventions continued to fail or to find no buyers. Even Edison, always so upbeat, began to sound discouraged. In response to a desperate letter from one of his (equally poor) coworkers back home, he wrote, "[N]o matter what I may do I reap nothing but trouble and the blues."

But even at this low point, his remarkable optimism shone through. "I'll never give up," he wrote, "because I may have a streak of luck before I die."

Edison had always intended to return to Boston once he'd raised some money in New York City. But he never did. Instead, he chose to start over, taking telegraphy jobs and continuing to invent in his spare time. Soon he had come up with new devices to improve telegraph operations and to help keep track of prices on the stock market.

By 1870, when Edison was just twenty-three, his inventions had begun to draw the attention of Western Union and other big companies. He even managed to sell the designs of some improvements in telegraphy, especially devices that would "read" codes on pieces of paper and send the messages down telegraph lines far faster than any person could. For the first time, he was able to put some money in the bank.

But this didn't mean life had gotten less hectic for the inventor (whose hair had already turned white). Between 1870 and 1875, Edison moved his shop several times. His mother died. He married a young woman named Mary Stillwell. He grew deeper in debt to companies that sold him supplies.

Tired of wandering, Edison decided that he needed a place he could truly call home, a place to live and work without having to put up with the noise and bother of the outside world. He was ready to settle down, to hire other inventors and assistants to work with him, and to pour all of his energy into his inventions.

In 1875 he found the place where he wanted to settle: a small farm in the quiet country town of Menlo Park, New Jersey, not far from the city of Newark and just a train ride away from New York. Here, Edison achieved a goal that must have been beyond his wildest dreams just a few years earlier: He got to design and build his own laboratory — and no one could take it away from him or kick him out of it. If he felt like setting the place on fire, dripping acid on the floor, or blowing it up, it was his decision and no one else's.

With Western Union paying most of the bills, Edison had a two-story building erected on the grounds of the old farm. One hundred feet long but only thirty feet wide, it was soon filled with chemicals, machines, books, and any device Edison and his assistants might ever have a need for. In many ways, it was the world's largest playroom for inventors, and Edison loved it from the first moment he set foot in it in 1876.

He loved it so much — and saw it as such a refuge from a noisy and interfering outside world — that he often would spend days on end there, even though his house was close by. He thought nothing of sleeping in the laboratory, surviving on countless cups of coffee and endless slices of pie.

Edison also wasted little time in building a team that would help him create the inventions that would make them all wealthy. Perhaps the two most important members of the team were men Edison had worked with for years, Charles Batchelor and John Kruesi. Batchelor understood machinery almost as well as Edison did, and was a far better draftsman, turning Edison's ideas into accu-

Edison with his daughter Marion and son Tom, Jr., and coworkers outside the laboratory at Menlo Park, around 1879–1880. After years of nearly constant movement from city to city, Edison settled in this rural area in New Jersey and allowed his mind to focus almost entirely on his inventions.

rate, detailed drawings. Kruesi took those drawings and turned them into reality, building devices that had the best possible chance of working.

It's a sign both of Edison's busy and eventful life, and of how much his team respected him, that soon after they set up shop, they gave him a new nickname: "Old Man." He wasn't even thirty years old.

While most of Edison's inventions before Menlo Park had focused on improving the telegraph, once he was settled in his new laboratory he began to think bigger. Hearing that Alexander Graham Bell and other inventors were experimenting with sending actual sounds — not just clicks and beeps — along electrical wires, Edison did the same. All these inventors thought that it might even be possible to send the sound of the human voice along a wire.

What they were all hoping to invent was the telephone. In working toward this goal, though, Edison ran into a problem that he had to face with many of his inventions: The people who were giving him money for his work (in this case, Western Union) couldn't understand why the invention was necessary. Even if he *could* design a telephone, officials at Western Union believed that the public wouldn't be very interested in it.

Edison turned his attention to another challenge: figuring out a way to record the human voice. By the end of 1877, he, Batchelor, and Kruesi had invented the first phonograph, which made and then "read" grooves in tinfoil to record and play back sounds. This device was a primitive version of the CD players we use today, which use laser light to "read" grooves in a plastic disk — but they're still doing pretty much what Edison's first phonograph did more than one hundred years ago.

Back in Edison's time, people were stunned by the invention. While those who worked with him still called him "Old Man," others came up with a new nickname for the young inventor: "The Wizard of Menlo Park."

But the Wizard was just getting started. After his first great accomplishment — the phonograph — he set his sights even higher.

Thomas Edison wanted to invent the lightbulb.

3
INVENTING THE LIGHTBULB

When you sit down to write a report, do you ever find that you have no idea how to begin?

You're not the only one to feel that way sometimes. Even a genius like Thomas Edison, who seemed to spend every minute of every day working on his inventions, often found himself unable to figure out what to do next. "In trying to perfect a thing, I sometimes run straight up against a granite wall a hundred feet high," he said.

But he wouldn't let these "walls" stop him. "I never allow myself to become discouraged under any circumstances," he said. This attitude was a necessity: While working on a new invention, he might try thousands of different ways to make it work, all of which would fail.

Once, an assistant got frustrated with this approach and said they should just give up, since they hadn't learned anything. Edison, though, thought his assistant was missing the point. "I cheerily assured him that we *had* learned something," he explained. "For we had learned with a certainty that the thing couldn't be done that way, and that we would have to try some other way."

We like to think of inventors sitting bolt upright in bed, shouting "Eureka!" and then rushing to the laboratory, where they quickly sketch out the cure for

Opposite
A model of the first successful lightbulb — seemingly so simple, but actually the result of countless frustrating hours in the laboratory.

cancer or the design of a rocket ship that can travel as fast as light. But this is not how most inventing actually takes place. Almost always, a brilliant new invention is the result of hard, hard work and countless failures. This was certainly true for Edison as he struggled for months to perfect the lightbulb.

Edison was far from the first inventor to try to design a light that worked through the principle of incandescence. Beginning in the early 1800s, hopeful inventors were constantly announcing that *they* were the ones who would create the first incandescent lamp. Today, their names — De la Rue, Grove, Jacobi, Adams, Osborn, Konn, Swan, Van Choate, Maxim, and others — have been forgotten, because they simply couldn't figure out how to make the lightbulb safe enough, bright enough, and cheap enough to produce.

They tried many clever variations. Many used small sticks of carbon, which glow brightly when they incandesce — but burn out quickly. Some put the carbon sticks in small glass containers, which they then sealed with metal caps, but the carbon still burned up quickly. Some added nitrogen gas to the containers, thinking that this might keep the carbon burning longer. Others had the smart idea that the carbon might not burn out so fast if they removed the air from the glass container (making a vacuum), but none were ever able to figure out how to make an adequate vacuum in a glass bulb.

Eventually, some inventors came to believe that it was impossible to keep carbon from burning so quickly and started to focus on designing ways to replace the burned-out carbon with a fresh stick. The problem was that it could take a trained worker two or three hours to put in a new carbon that might last only a few minutes. If your bulb blew out, the worker would barely have time to leave your house before he had to come back and replace the carbon again — you might as well just give him a room to sleep in.

These inventors' failures gave Edison and his assistants some hints about what a successful lightbulb must be able to do. "To be adapted to domestic use it must be simple, and of light weight," Francis Jehl wrote in his book, *Menlo Park Reminiscences*. "Furthermore it must be flexible and must function under

all conditions and in all positions. It must be cheap. Its flame must be noiseless and inoffensive." And, most important of all, it must give steady and bright light for hours at a time.

That was a lot of "musts" — but if anyone was equipped to solve the problems, Thomas Edison was. He'd done a few experiments with lightbulb carbons in 1877 but had stopped to work on the phonograph. By September of 1878, he was ready to put all of his brilliant imagination into the job of building a better lightbulb.

Within just a few weeks, he was sure he could do it — and do it right. In an interview with the *New York Sun* on October 10, 1878, he sounded completely confident. When the reporter asked him if he was sure that he could build a light that would be better and cheaper than gas lamps, Edison's answer was "There can be no doubt of it."

The Holmes Magneto Electric Light Apparatus, as exhibited in 1862: An early example of arc lighting, and exactly the sort of unwieldy, expensive light source that Edison hoped to replace with his electric lamp.

"Will it be an electric light?" the reporter asked.

"Electricity and nothing else," said the inventor.

Then he went on to describe how the lightbulb would work. Matches wouldn't be needed to light it. It could be turned on or off at any time. It would provide a white, steady light, it would give off no smoke, and it would never explode. People would even be able to move their electric lamps from one place to another — something that was never possible with permanently attached gas lamps.

To some scientists, Edison's predictions seemed ridiculous. One, a man named Professor Sylvanus Thompson, went so far as to accuse Edison of having "the most airy ignorance" of the basic principles of electricity.

What did Edison think of such criticisms? Not much. On October 15, 1878, he created the Edison Electric Light Company, located at the laboratories in Menlo Park. Many of the others working in the new company were the same people who had collaborated with Edison on the phonograph and some of his other inventions.

Making the lightbulb a reality would prove to be a harder job than even Edison could have guessed. He had optimistically predicted that he would invent a working lightbulb in just six weeks. As it turned out, the Wizard of Menlo Park and his brilliant staff worked long days and seven-day weeks for more than a year before they solved the problems that had stopped so many earlier inventors.

"The electric light has caused me the greatest amount of study," Edison said later. "I was never myself discouraged, or inclined to be hopeless of success. I cannot say the same for all of my associates."

Edison and his team faced challenges we have trouble imagining today. We can buy a box of lightbulbs in the store, open it, and find each bulb exactly the same, each perfect. But there were no factories making the glass bulbs in Edison's time — and before he could even assume that he could create a working electric light, he had to have the bulbs themselves to experiment on.

Opposite
Edison (far left, seated) with his staff at the Menlo Park laboratories, the birthplace of the lightbulb and the center of American invention for decades.

MACHINE SHOP.

He did this by hiring a man named Ludwig Boehm, who was an expert glassblower. "Blowing" glass meant dipping the end of a long pipe into a bucket of molten glass, capturing a dripping ball of the liquid on the end of the pipe, and then gently blowing into the other end. Slowly, as the glass cooled and became harder, Boehm would blow it into the shape of a small globe, much as you might inflate a balloon.

But the slightest false move, the slightest weakness in one wall of the hot and gooey bulb would make it pop, becoming nothing more than a lump of useless glass. Back into the bucket of molten glass it would go, and Boehm would patiently try again. Usually, though, he succeeded, providing Edison with enough bulbs to experiment on.

Next came the problem of removing the air from the bulbs — making a vacuum, which Edison was sure was the secret to having the carbon shine more brightly and last longer. Luckily, at the same time that Edison began working on the lightbulb, other inventors were building vacuum pumps, machines

designed to suck the air out of containers. Edison bought a few of these, adapted them to his needs, and set them up in his Menlo Park laboratory.

The biggest challenge facing the Edison Electric Light Company team was finding a carbon that would incandesce without burning out after just a few seconds or minutes. Since almost any substance will incandesce if you run enough electric current through it, Edison turned away from the sticks of carbon previous inventors had used. He decided to try other materials — just about anything he could think of.

The laboratory at Menlo Park, Francis Jehl reported, was soon lined with jars filled with "horsehair, fish line, teak, spruce, boxwood, vulcanized rubber, cork, celluloid, grass fibers from everywhere, linen twine, tar paper, wrapping paper, cardboard, tissue paper, parchment, holly wood, absorbent cotton, rattan, California redwood," gold, platinum, and other materials. Edison even tried a strand from a spider web, which glowed with a green light before it burned up.

The search for a new, better carbon (which Edison renamed the "filament") even grew into a contest among the workers at Menlo Park. Edison decided to try human hair — and his choice was hair plucked from the beards of two members of his team, John Kruesi and James MacKenzie. Kruesi, Francis Jehl explained, was "a cool mountaineer from Switzerland possessed of a bushy black beard," while MacKenzie's hairs "were stiff and bristling."

Everyone gathered to see which hair would incandesce longer. "Bets were placed with much gusto by the supporters of the men," said Jehl, "and many arguments held over the rival merits of their beards."

As it turned out, MacKenzie's beard lasted longer under the electric current than did Kruesi's. This result was rejected by Kruesi's supporters, who claimed that their man's beard hair had been subjected to a stronger electric current. True or not, neither man's beard ultimately provided the filament that would make the lightbulb work.

The process of testing each filament was terribly slow and frustrating. After

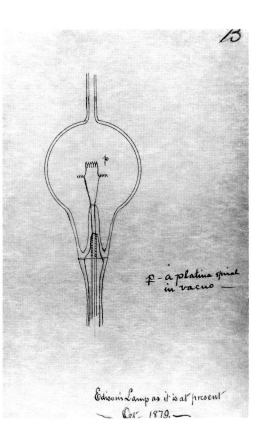

Left
If at first you don't succeed: Edison's sketches of possible designs for the lightbulb's wiring and filament.

Above
A sketch of a bulb with a platinum filament, tested in October 1879. The work, said Edison's co-worker Francis Jehl, was "tedious, backbreaking, and heartbreaking."

Feb 13 1880.

Large globe small horseshoe

Tin foil

Carbon coated with an oxide, say alumina or lime.

a substance was chosen, a piece had to be made as thin as a hair (unless it was one already!). Then it had to be carbonized (baked in an oven without oxygen until it was charred), since Edison believed that carbonized filaments would incandesce longer and more brightly.

The hardest part came next. The filament had to be attached to thin platinum wires, so electric current could be run through it. The ends of the wires had to be inserted into a still-soft glass stem, freshly made by Ludwig Boehm. The stem, one end of a pair of long wires, and the filament then had to be inserted inside the fragile bulb itself. The whole construction was placed atop a vacuum pump and then sealed after the air was removed from the bulb.

Many, many times, the filament, bulb, or stem broke during this process, and it was not possible to test the filament unless all the pieces stayed intact. Of course, even then the filaments almost never worked — they wouldn't produce a bright enough light, or they'd burn up immediately. Edison would make

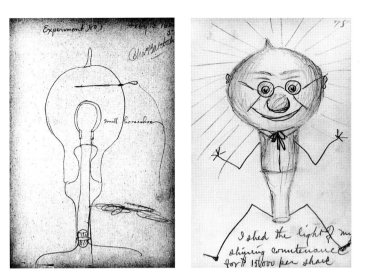

a note on a piece of paper, and then he and his team had to start the whole process all over again with the next filament. Francis Jehl called the work "tedious, backbreaking, and heartbreaking."

But Edison and the others at Menlo Park didn't give up, and by October of 1879 all their faith and hard work finally began to show some rewards. Amazingly, after all the odd substances he had tried as filaments, Edison found that what worked best was a simple piece of carbonized cotton thread.

There are various versions of this story, but Francis Jehl wrote that as he and Edison watched a lightbulb glow one October night, they thought they were simply waiting the usual few minutes before the cotton filament burned out. As the hours passed, however, and the filament kept glowing brightly, they began to realize that the challenge of the lightbulb had finally been solved.

The bulb kept burning all that night and all the next day — in fact, until midafternoon of the day after that, more than forty hours after it had been lit.

Edison's lightbulb in 1880. This photo of a "carbon-horseshoe lamp" clearly shows the platinum screw clamps and lead-in wires.

According to Jehl, Edison's comment was, "If it will burn that number of hours now, I know I can make it burn a hundred!" Finally, the great inventor could see a future in which the lightbulb would illuminate homes and other buildings across the world.

From that moment on, Edison never looked back. Almost immediately, he began planning a big public exhibition of his electric light, but until the exhibition was ready, he kept news of his invention under wraps, not letting newspaper reporters into Menlo Park. At the same time, he continued improving the lightbulb, replacing the carbonized cotton thread he'd used as a filament with a horseshoe-shaped piece of carbonized cardboard, which seemed to burn even longer and more steadily.

In early December, Edison used lightbulbs to illuminate his own house and that of the scientist Francis R. Upton, who had worked closely with him in creating the lightbulb. "There will be a great sensation when the light is made known to the world," Upton wrote to his father on December 7, 1879, "for it does so much more than anyone expects can be done."

By now the world had begun to realize that something big had happened at Menlo Park, but still Edison waited. He wanted the unveiling of his invention to be perfect — and he also knew that the longer he waited, the more excited the public would be.

In the middle of the month, reporters (especially the one from the *New York Herald*, who practically lived at Menlo Park that December) began hearing about successful demonstrations of the electric light. Stories were told of groups of important bankers, scientists, investors in the Edison Electric Light Company, and others visiting the laboratory. All the stories seemed to say that the visitors left excited and pleased by what they had seen.

Still, not everyone was convinced. One Henry Morton, a professor at the Stevens Institute of Technology in New Jersey, made the mistake of expressing his doubts publicly. Without having visited Menlo Park, he called the electric light "a conspicuous failure" and a "fraud upon the public."

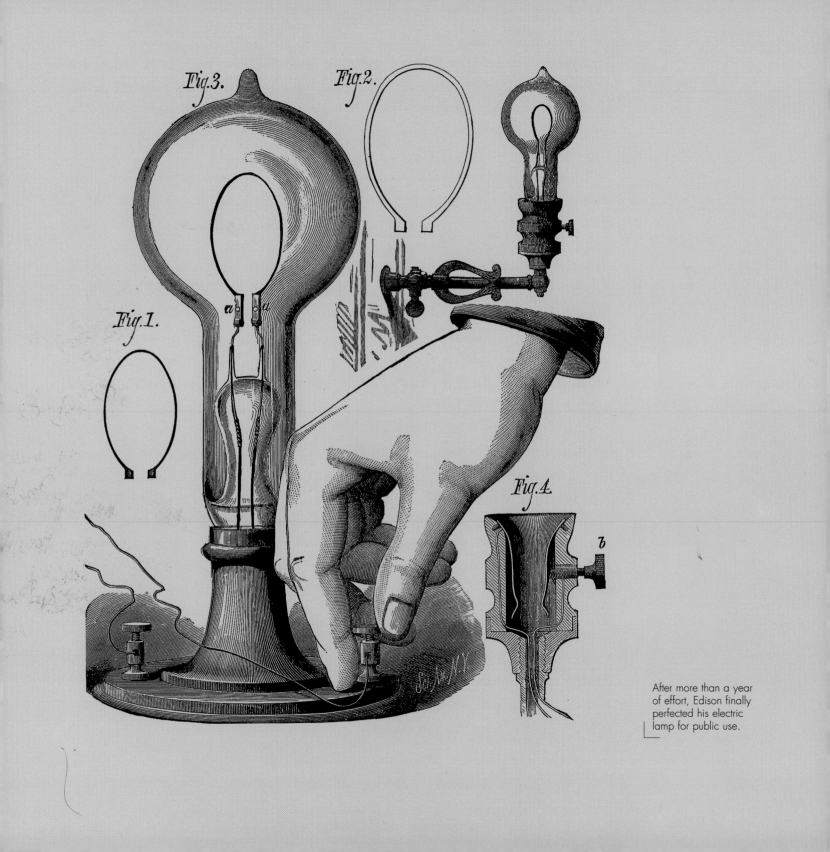

Fig.3.   Fig.2.

Fig.1.

Fig.4.

After more than a year
of effort, Edison finally
perfected his electric
lamp for public use.

It's easy to see why Professor Morton and others found it hard to believe that Edison had succeeded where so many others had failed. For many years, most scientists had assumed — and said out loud — that gaslight was what people would always use to illuminate their houses. They didn't want Edison to prove them wrong.

Unlike these last few doubters, the editors of the *Herald* were able to look ahead and see what the future would hold. "If [the electric light] is a better, purer, more manageable, cleanlier, and, above all, a cheaper light than gas, then gas is doomed," they wrote.

For most people, there were no "ifs" about it. They were ready to believe that Thomas Edison and his assistant wizards at Menlo Park were creating a miracle. And the public grew even more excited after reading Marshall Fox's article in the *Herald* on December 21. Edison's new lamps, Fox wrote, shone with "a tiny beautiful light, like the mellow sunset of an Italian autumn." It was, he added, "a light that is like a little globe of sunshine, a veritable Aladdin's lamp."

Then, finally, on New Year's Eve, the public got its first look at what all the fuss was about. Edison threw open the doors of Menlo Park and invited everyone to come see what he, Jehl, Upton, and the rest of the team had been working on for so many months.

So many people took Edison up on his offer that the railroad had to add more trains from nearby cities to Menlo Park. Three thousand people visited that one evening, and what they saw amazed them. "The laboratory was brightly illuminated with twenty-five electric lamps, the office and counting room with eight, and twenty others were distributed in the street leading to the depot and in some of the adjoining houses," wrote Marshall Fox.

Watching these bulbs glow steadily, brilliantly, for hours, no one could doubt that Edison had succeeded. The lightbulb was no longer just a dream; it was a reality. It was, as one magazine wrote after the New Year's Eve demonstration, "A New Light to the World."

FROM THE POWER PLANT TO YOUR LIGHTBULB

Whenever you turn on a light, you use electricity that was generated at a power plant. Most power plants produce electricity by harnessing the energy from moving water or steam. Steam is created when water is heated to boiling by burning coal, gas, oil, or garbage, or during nuclear reactions. Other power plants harness the power of the sun or the wind.

Electricity moves along wires out of the power plant and eventually all the way to your house, as well as to streets, office buildings, and anywhere else that needs it.

A switch lets you turn the flow of electricity on and off.

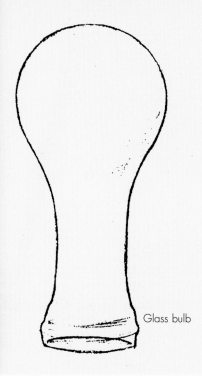

Glass bulb

E: The air is sucked out of the bulb through the exhaust tube, and the tube is heated, cut off, and fused closed. Removing the air from the bulb prevents the filament from quickly burning out. Today, bulbs usually contain a gas (such as argon) that prevents the filament from combining with any oxygen that may be left in the bulb, and burning out.

F: Finally, the base is baked on, and the lead wires are separated. One is soldered to the upper edge of the threaded base, and the other is poked through a hole in the insulated button on the bottom of the base and secured with a blob of solder.

E

F

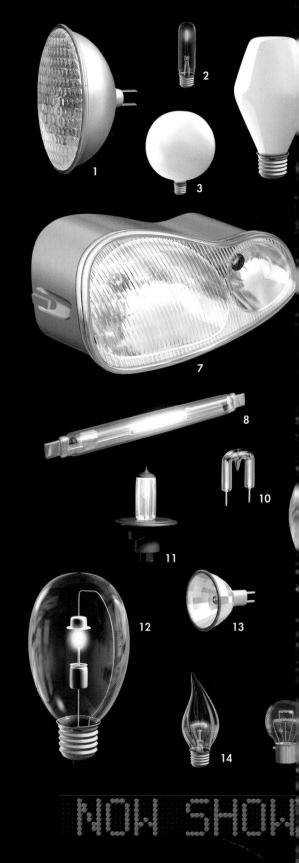

1

2

3

7

8

10

11

12

13

14

PUTTING THE PARTS TOGETHER

A: The lead wires are placed through the flare.

B: The glass exhaust tube and flare are heated and fused together to form a seal and hold the lead wires. A hole is made through the top of the fused area into the exhaust tube.

C: The anchor wires and support wire are fused to the top end of the exhaust tube, and the anchor wires are wound around the lead wires for stability. Then the filament is attached to the top ends of the lead wires, and the support wire is wound loosely around the thin filament to hold it gently.

D: The bulb is placed over this assembly. Its bottom is heated and narrowed and then fused with the bottom of the flare. Now the bulb is sealed except for the small hole through the exhaust tube.

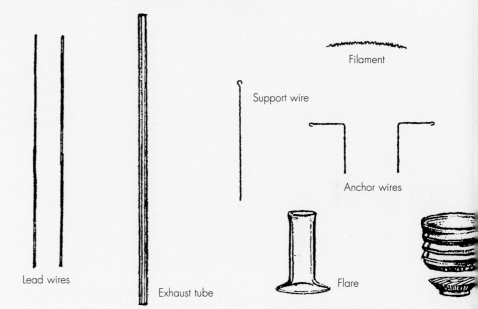

Lead wires

Exhaust tube

Filament

Support wire

Anchor wires

Flare

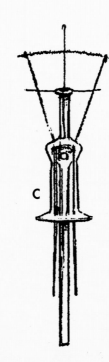

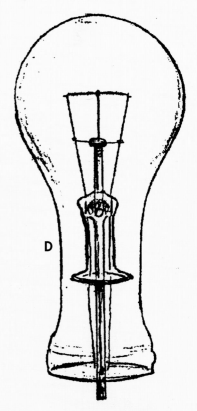

A

B

C

D

A LIGHTBULB'S PARTS

Filament. Today, this is made of a tightly coiled metal wire made of tungsten.

Anchor wires hold the filament in place.

Flare, through which two wires — the lead wires — run from the base of the bulb to the filament.

Exhaust tube, a space through which the air is sucked out of the bulb to make a vacuum.

Glass bulb, mass-produced by the billions today.

Base, which in modern bulbs is threaded to allow us to screw light-bulbs into lamps and light fixtures.

Lead wires carry electricity into the bulb. Connections from the end of the lead wires to the base allow the electricity generated in a power plant to enter a lightbulb.

MANY SHAPES FOR MANY USES

1. Lantern light
2. High-intensity bulb
3. Globe bulb
4. Energy-saving bulb
5. Outdoor floodlight
6. Tubular bulb
7. Car headlight
8. Halogen straight bulb
9. Mercury vapor bulb
10. Xenon strobe light
11. Halogen H4 car bulb
12. Halogen arc lamp
13. Halogen projector lamp
14. Flame-style bulb
15. Car turn-signal bulb
16. Light-emitting diode
17. Lighted strip sign

From the smallest lightbulb — a "wheat grain" lamp used in model railroading — to the largest — an airport landing light.

EDISON'S FIRST LIGHTBULB

After a long search, Edison found that carbonized cotton thread made the best, longest-burning filaments in the first lightbulbs.

In 1929, the fiftieth anniversary of the lightbulb's invention, Francis Jehl and Thomas Edison re-created their experiments in a reconstruction of the Menlo Park laboratories in Greenfield Village, Dearborn, Michigan. Edison enjoyed the visit thoroughly but complained of the rebuilt room: "We never kept it as clean as this!"

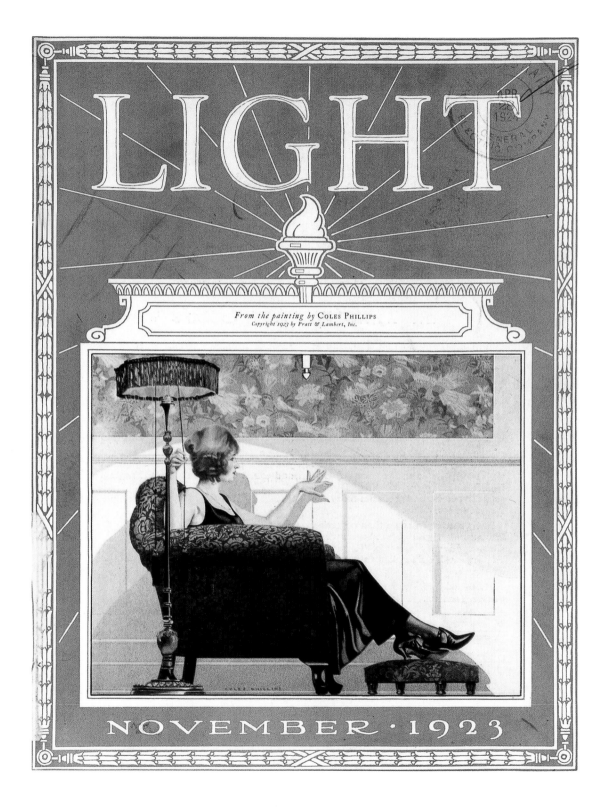

LIGHT

From the painting by COLES PHILLIPS
Copyright 1923 by Pratt & Lambert, Inc.

NOVEMBER · 1923

4

A REVOLUTION OF LIGHT

Edison showed on New Year's Eve, 1879, that he could illuminate his laboratory and some nearby buildings. But what would he do with the lightbulb next? Could he actually make it a successful commercial product, lighting office buildings and people's houses, or would it always be just a toy, an object to marvel at in museums and fairs?

Edison knew he had a big job ahead of him if he was to prove that the lightbulb would work just as well elsewhere as it did in Menlo Park. Despite all the newspaper headlines calling him a wizard, to him the lightbulb would be a failure if it didn't gain wide acceptance.

Thomas Edison had to convince people that they *wanted* his new electric light — that they wanted to let electricity itself into their homes and buildings. Remember, in 1879 most people had never come into contact with a single device that used electricity. At most, they may have seen a generator producing electricity to power an arc lamp, but the idea that their houses might one day be supplied with electricity over a network of wires was completely strange to them — strange and a bit scary. People knew that electricity was dangerous: It could hurt or even kill you.

So Edison had to lessen people's fear and distrust of electricity and con-

Opposite
With the pull of a string or, later, the flip of a switch, you could fill an entire room with light thanks to Edison's invention. The lightbulb made it easy to create light almost anywhere.

vince them instead that it was a wonderful tool to light their homes. Just as importantly, he also had to create a way to get electricity to the streets and buildings he planned to light up.

To achieve these goals, he had to:

- Figure out a way to reliably distribute electrical current to hundreds or thousands of buildings at once. It was important, Edison wrote, that "in any given city area the lights could be fed with electricity from several directions, thus eliminating any interruption due to disturbance on any particular section."
- Build a lightbulb that gave out as much light as a gas lamp, while costing less. The electric light, Edison added, "must be durable, capable of being easily and safely handled by the public, and . . . remain capable of burning at full incandescence and candle power a great length of time."
- Develop a meter to measure the amount of electricity being used by each customer so that customers could be charged accordingly.
- Design a system of electrical wires that could be placed on poles or in pipes underground and run into each building that used electric lights.
- Come up with devices (called regulators) to keep the electric current from the power source constant. This was important so the lightbulbs "wherever located, near or far away from the central station, should give an equal light at all times." Regulators would also make sure that the bulbs wouldn't "rupture by sudden and violent fluctuations of current."
- Design efficient generators to produce the electricity that would be needed by the countless thousands of lightbulbs Edison dreamed of selling to the public.
- Invent new devices to make electric light safe and easy to use, especially safety devices that would prevent fires or electric shocks. New inventions had to include "switches for turning the current on and off; lampholders, fixtures [sockets], and the like; also means and methods for establishing the interior circuits that were to carry current to chandeliers and fixtures in buildings."

Edison realized from the very start that electric light was merely the tip of

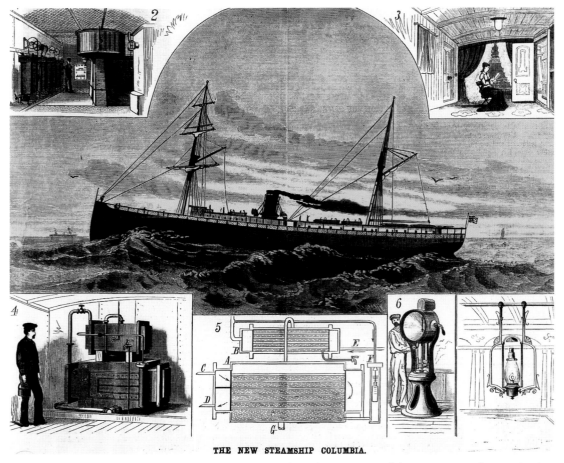

THE NEW STEAMSHIP COLUMBIA.

the iceberg. Once it had reached people's homes and businesses through the wires he would install, electricity would have many other uses. In addition to the electric light, Edison predicted that someday people would use electric elevators, printing presses, lathes, fans, and other devices that did not yet exist.

In early 1880, as Edison and his team set to work on the huge task of making the electric light available to the public, an exciting opportunity came their way. One of their financial supporters, Henry Villard, the head of a shipping company, asked Edison to install a system of electric lights on his new steamship, *Columbia*.

Edison thought this was a good idea. Lighting a ship would be like lighting

The first test of a lighting system using the light-bulb didn't take place in buildings, but on the steamship *Columbia*, which carried four generators and 150 electric lights — and drew crowds wherever it docked in 1880.

a small neighborhood, but under very controlled, self-contained conditions. It would give him the chance to test a lighting system larger than any available at Menlo Park, without risking the bad publicity that would come from a failed attempt in a real city neighborhood.

To design *Columbia's* lighting, Edison had to begin tackling some of the related devices he had known would be necessary to make the lightbulb a commercial success. Probably the most important of these was some kind of switch that would shut off the electricity in case of an accidental surge. In other words, Edison had to invent the world's first fuse or circuit breaker. He settled on what he called "safety wires," which melted when overloaded with electricity.

Columbia, outfitted with four generators and 150 electric lights, sailed from New York City on May 9, 1880 — less than five months after Edison's first pub-

From the start, Edison dreamed of mass-production of his light-bulb — and, as these pictures from a factory in 1903 show, his dream was to be realized.

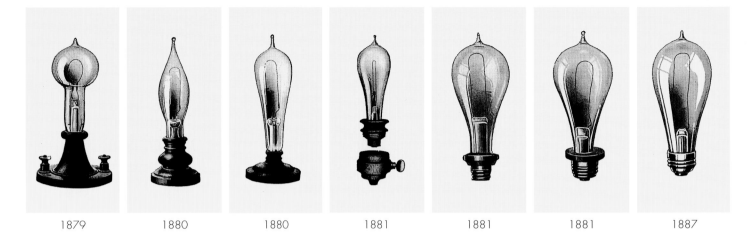

1879   1880   1880   1881   1881   1881   1887

lic display of the lightbulb. It must have made a spectacular impression, with the warm light of Edison's lightbulbs glowing from its decks and portholes. As the ship made its way south, stopping in ports along the way, people flocked to visit it, and Edison's fame grew even larger. He'd shown that the lightbulb could work outside Menlo Park.

Edison's next step was clear: to design a system that could illuminate cities. He decided to start with a single neighborhood, but even this meant building a power plant with generators on a far larger scale than any before, as well as sending wires into dozens of homes and businesses.

Edison's choice was to light part of New York City. He first dreamed of lighting all of lower Manhattan. Imagine the glory, great publicity, and financial rewards that would have followed the illumination of such a huge area! But the truth was that the Edison Electric Light Company didn't have the money, the workforce, or the time to build such a large system.

Instead, Edison chose the First District, a ten-by-ten-block area just north of Manhattan's famous Wall Street. Even this was a big job. Edison used an entire building, on Pearl Street, to house the steam engines, boilers, and enormous generators — the most powerful ever built — that would send electricity down the wires to light up the buildings of the First District. Workers had to string

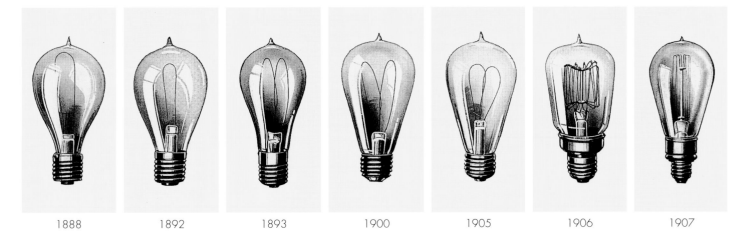

| 1888 | 1892 | 1893 | 1900 | 1905 | 1906 | 1907 |

some wires from telegraph poles, dig up streets to run other wires underground, and then snake them all up into buildings.

If Menlo Park had seemed busy during the months spent perfecting the light-bulb, now it became even more hectic and crowded. Edison and more than sixty coworkers struggled to solve all the problems that might result from installing electric lights in a city neighborhood.

Finally, on September 4, 1882, Edison was ready to show the world that his electric light was more than just an interesting curiosity. Standing in the office of the millionaire businessman J. P. Morgan, Edison himself flicked the switches that turned on the offices' lamps. Then, one by one, more than two dozen buildings followed, until more than eight hundred lightbulbs were illuminated across the First District.

"In stores and business places throughout the lower quarters of the city there was a strange glow last night," reported the *New York Herald*. "The dim flicker of gas . . . was supplanted by a steady glare, bright and mellow, which illuminated interiors and shone through windows fixed and unwavering."

Edison himself watched this great success with quiet satisfaction. His comment to a newspaper reporter was simple: "I have accomplished all I promised," he said.

The evolution of the lightbulb, 1879–1907. Gradual changes in the design of the filament and lead-in wires, the introduction and perfection of the screw base, and other improvements helped bring the bulb into nearly every home.

Even after this dramatic demonstration, widespread public acceptance of the electric light took years. But by 1900 more than 25 million incandescent lights had been sold in the United States. More and more people were abandoning gas and other light sources and turning to the cheaper, better lightbulb.

Once other scientists and inventors saw how electricity could be controlled and used to light something as small and fragile as a lightbulb, they began looking for other uses

for electric power. By the early 1900s, many of the technological leaps forward that Edison had long imagined — and some even he had never thought of — were becoming a reality.

In 1907, for example, the Brooklyn Edison Company built and showed off the "house of the future." It contained an oven, dishwasher, refrigerator (with built-in icemaker), iron, washing machine, vacuum cleaner, and other devices — all powered by electricity. In many ways, in fact, 1907's house of the future was our house of today.

Edison's lightbulb was the first small step toward making that house a reality, the first of a series of technological advances that forever changed the way we live. Air conditioners, televisions, and computers are all just further steps in that journey, a journey that will never end, as scientists and inventors keep studying electricity's uses.

These pages
What Edison foresaw: the easy-to-use, inexpensive, and bright lightbulb, in use in homes and businesses around the world.

Pages 66–67
The dazzling sight of the Eiffel Tower, illuminated by electric light, in Paris in 1900; turning night into day in New York City's Times Square, 1927; the Las Vegas strip today — lighting the darkness with billions of electric lights.

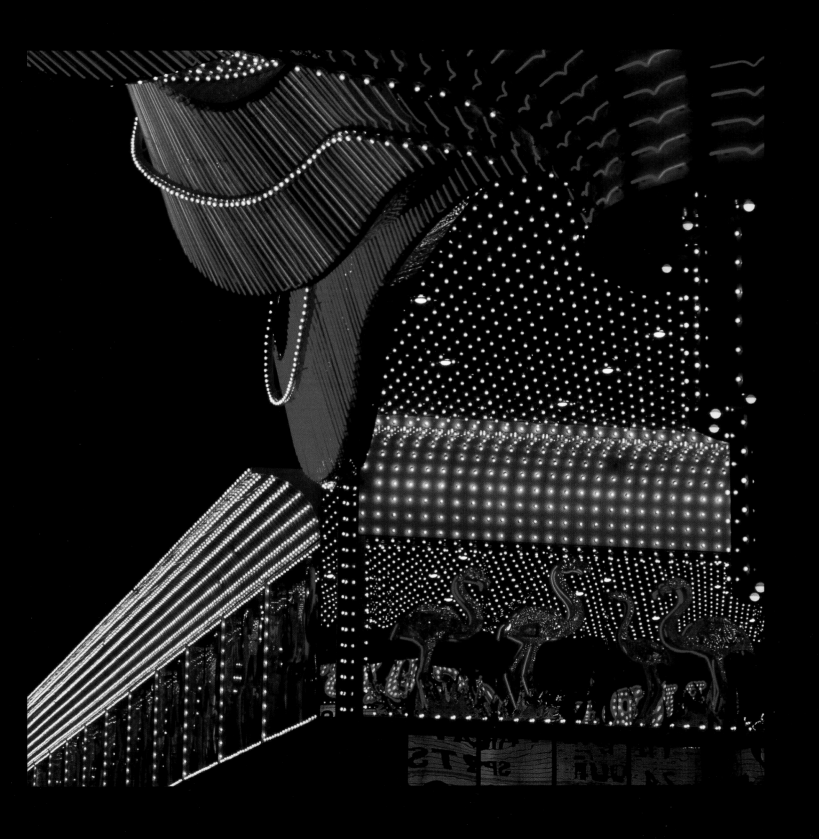

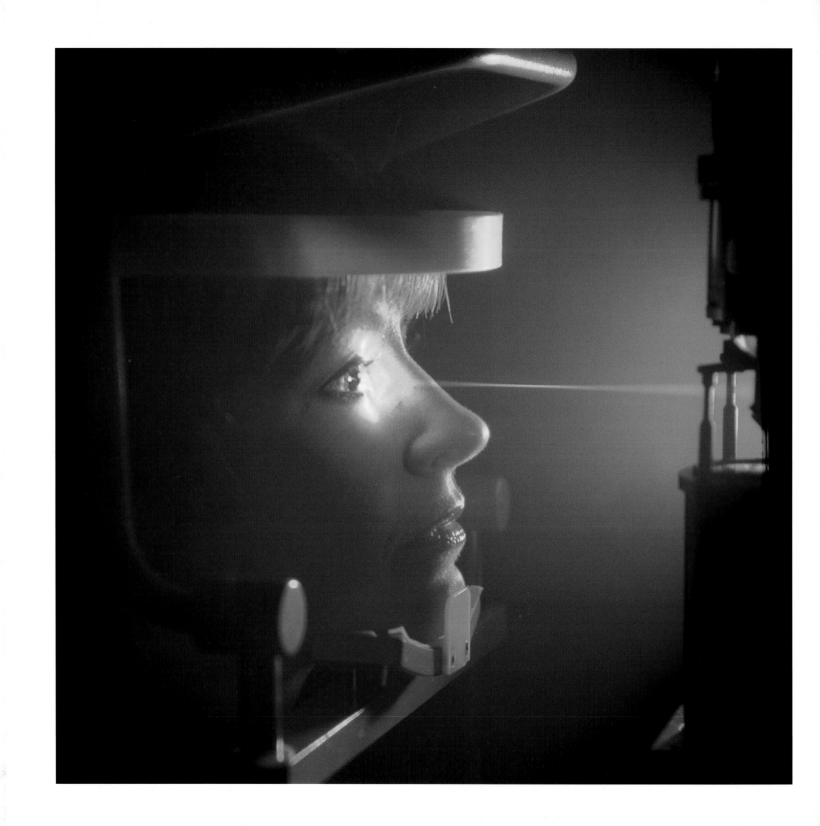

5
THE FUTURE OF LIGHT

Thomas Edison dreamed that his lightbulb would someday illuminate buildings across the world, and by the time he died in 1931, he'd lived long enough to see that dream come true. Throughout his life, he also saw advances in other ways to light a room, a street, or a sign.

Perhaps the best-known lighting alternative is the fluorescent tube. As long ago as 1867 — twelve years before Edison perfected his lightbulb — a French scientist named A. E. Becquerel had created the first fluorescent bulb, one very similar to those we see in homes and offices today.

What makes fluorescent bulbs light up is a surprising series of chemical reactions. The long, slender bulbs contain a small amount of mercury and are coated on the inside with a white fluorescent powder. When you flick a switch on, an electric current enters the bulb. The current heats the mercury, which turns into gas and emits rays of ultraviolet light. But this isn't the light we see when the bulb lights up. (Ultraviolet light is invisible to our eyes.) Instead, the ultraviolet rays are absorbed by the powder, which then fluoresces — it glows, producing the familiar bluish light we can actually see.

Today, not all bulbs that use the concept of fluorescence produce this cool, blue-white light. Streetlights often contain sodium vapor, which glows bright

yellow-orange when exposed to an electric current. So-called neon lights actually can contain any of a number of gases, depending on what color the designer wants the bulbs to produce. (A bulb containing neon alone will create only red light.) Halogen lamps operate in a similar fashion to produce their hot, bright glow.

A light-emitting diode (LED), another source of illumination, is a tiny electronic device that produces light as electric current passes through it. We are all familiar with LED displays on clock radios and other electronic equipment today, but in the future they may be used for car headlights and even — as huge, flat panels mounted on walls — for room lighting.

As varied as these developments in light are, they all deal with illumination. Remarkably, however, there are now many other uses of light. One example is the laser, which emits a tightly focused, intense beam of light so powerful that it can cut through steel and so precise that it can remove tumors during the most delicate surgery. Today, lasers are commonly used everywhere from factories and operating rooms to rock concerts, where their bright beams add to the show. Researchers are investigating many other possible uses for laser light, such as communication — a laser beam would carry a signal like a radio transmission sent through the air.

But well before laser phones become a reality, laser light may help bring the virtual retinal display (VRD) into our lives. This remarkable invention sends visual information from a computer to a pair of lenses worn in front of a person's eyes. With the help of special computer programs and a pair of moving

Lighting alternatives to the incandescent bulb: fluorescent tubes (like this one from 1941, *above*) and compact fluorescent bulbs (*opposite*), in wide use in office buildings today.

mirrors, that information is then "sketched" directly onto the eyes by lasers. As a result, the person can see the sketched images more clearly than if he or she were watching them on a screen.

When this device is perfected, it will mean that people will no longer have to clutter their homes and offices with television screens and computer monitors. To watch a movie or play a computer game, they'll simply put on their VRD glasses. The same technology — an improvement over virtual-reality flight simulators — will be used to train fighter pilots by broadcasting realistic combat scenes directly onto their eyes during training. The U.S. Air Force and private companies are already planning to install VRD in helicopters and jets.

But perhaps the most exciting use for VRD will be in operating rooms. By projecting a cancer patient's X-rays directly on a surgeon's eyes, VRD will provide a "map" of a patient's tumor. It will also show surrounding healthy areas, the location of important blood vessels, and other crucial data that will make an operation easier to perform.

What goes on in some operating rooms has already changed due to another form of light, one that can help the surgeons repair injuries. Let's say that you're running, and you fall and hurt your knee so badly that you need surgery. In the past, this would have meant that surgeons would make a large cut in the surface of your knee, an incision long enough to enable them to see the injury inside and repair it. Then after the operation, you'd have to spend a week or more in the hospital so that you could recover not just from the injury, but from the damage done by the surgery itself.

Recently, though, researchers have found a new way to perform some kinds of surgery, thanks to light. The answer is called fiber optics. This technology involves sending light through the inside of an extremely thin cable (sometimes no thicker than a wire) made of pure glass. The glass is so pure that no light escapes, no matter how long the cable is or how much it is bent or twisted. This and the glass's other qualities make it possible for the light to stay strong and bright until it comes out the other end of the cable.

Doctors use fiber optics in amazing ways during surgery. They have designed flexible tubes (called endoscopes or laparoscopes) sometimes no more than an inch across that contain fiber-optic cables, miniature video cameras, and small surgical instruments for cutting, cleaning, and even stitching up an injury.

Today, if you hurt your knee, doctors won't necessarily have to make a large incision, but instead may take care of it using a laparoscope. The bright light flowing through the fiber-optic cable will let the video camera send back a clear view of the problem to a monitor for the doctors to study. Then, using the image on the screen and computers to help guide the instruments, the surgeons do all the repair work that's necessary. After removing the laparoscope, all they have to do is stitch up the inch-long incision they made. In many cases,

The extremely tightly focused beams of laser light are used for everything from communication to delicate surgery to etching patterns on computer chips. Someday, they may even help us launch rockets into space.

FLASH IS
PLACED UNDER
GIANT PENETRO-
ELECTRODES. THE   4-16-39
HEAT BECOMES UNBEARABLE. SUDDENLY,
ZARKOV SHOUTS--"ENOUGH! HE'S
BREATHING --HE'S BREATHING!"

NEXT WEEK:-- DEATH STALKS AGAIN

A forerunner of the laser: In 1939 Flash Gordon, covered in ice, is brought back to life by a powerful beam of light.

a patient undergoing knee surgery can be out of the hospital after just one day and be able to return to school or work within a few days.

In just a few years, doctors have gone from fixing knees and other joints to removing appendixes to repairing hernias using laparoscopes. They hope someday to be able to perform almost all surgeries in this way — to make old-fashioned open surgery as unnecessary as the gas lamp became after Edison invented his electric light.

Light has many other uses in medicine. One exciting discovery is that bright light itself can cure certain medical problems. This kind of treatment, called phototherapy, is already an important tool for treating a serious condition called jaundice that can occur in newborn babies, and it also combats a form of depression that can strike during the winter when people have relatively little exposure to sunlight. People with this condition sit in front of special "light boxes," usually for a couple of hours a day. During this time, they can read, write, talk on the phone — what's important is that the bright light shines on their faces for long enough to have an effect. People who undergo light therapy for this form of depression report feeling much happier and calmer, even on the worst winter days. For them, light brings happiness.

In the future, phototherapy may be a good tool in fighting such serious illnesses as cancer. Researchers have found that some cancerous tumors shrink — meaning their cells begin to die — when exposed to bright light. Someday, cancers that are now thought to be untreatable may respond to phototherapy.

The frontiers of medicine are not the only ones being explored by offspring of the first electric light. Using light, scientists have been able to investigate a mysterious world that usually exists in total darkness far beyond the reach of the sun, in the ocean's depths. The spotlights shone by high-tech research submarines called submersibles have changed our understanding of life on earth. They've shown us an incredible assortment of creatures that, in the absence of sunlight, make their own flickering, cold light, called bioluminescence. And they've even introduced us to amazing creatures that live on the seafloor thousands of feet down — giant worms, clams, and fish that can stand cold, lack of oxygen, and water pressures far greater than any we could have imagined. Robot submersibles operated from ships floating on the surface travel into deep undersea canyons and explore the hulls of the *Titanic* and other sunken ships, sending back spectacular images we would never see in any other way.

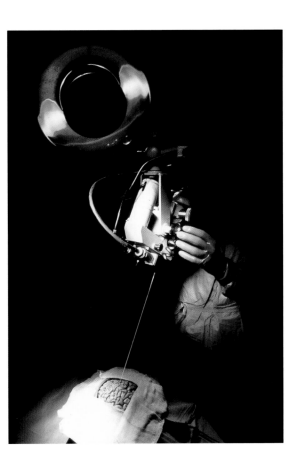

While some researchers are exploring the darkest corners of our planet, others are using Edison's invention to light a path away from the earth itself. The electric light, in freeing us from depending on the sun or such dangerous light sources as gas and candles, has allowed us to place men and women in airtight spacecraft traveling through the endless darkness of space. Without artificial light, there could be no space exploration, no space station, and certainly no colonization of other planets.

And now it seems that light may make space exploration far easier and more productive in an entirely different way: Light itself may one day launch rockets into space.

Today, one of the toughest challenges of space flight is that rockets need a vast quantity of fuel in order to achieve liftoff. Fuel is heavy — in fact, up to 90 percent of a rocket's weight is taken up by the fuel it needs to power its flight into space.

But scientists are building a rocket that won't need nearly as much fuel, for

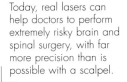

Today, real lasers can help doctors to perform extremely risky brain and spinal surgery, with far more precision than is possible with a scalpel.

this new rocket will be sent into space by the power of laser light. It's actually pretty simple: The bottom of the spacecraft will be made of highly polished metal. When the beam of a laser is aimed at it, it will act as a mirror, reflecting and focusing the beam into the air directly beneath the craft. This focused light will be so intense and powerful that it will quickly heat small patches of air to an astounding 54,000 degrees Fahrenheit, creating clouds of gas called plasma. At this heat, the gas clouds will suddenly explode, producing bursts of energy powerful enough to send the craft into space.

Space exploration was surely the last thing on Thomas Edison's mind as he struggled to find a working filament for his lightbulb. More than a hundred years later, though, we can see that he did more than help us light our rooms more efficiently. In countless ways, he not only made life as we know it possible, but he also helped create our future.

FURTHER READING

Adair, Gene. *Edison: Inventing the Electric Age*. New York: Oxford University Press, 1996.

Baldwin, Neil. *Edison: Inventing the Century*. New York: Hyperion, 1995.

Clark, Ronald W. *Edison: The Man Who Made the Future*. New York: Putnam, 1977.

Conot, Robert. *A Streak of Luck*. New York: Simon & Schuster, 1979.

Cosner, Shaaron. *The Light Bulb*. New York: Walker, 1984.

Ford, Henry, with Samuel Crowther. *Edison As I Know Him*. New York: Cosmopolitan Book Corp., 1930.

Friedel, Robert D., and Paul Israel with Bernard S. Finn. *Edison's Electric Light: Biography of an Invention*. New Brunswick, N.J.: Rutgers University Press, 1986.

Jehl, Francis. *Menlo Park Reminiscences*. New York: Dover, 1990. (Originally published in 1936.)

McClure, J. B. *Edison and His Inventions*. New York: Rhodes & McClure, 1891.

Van de Water, Marjorie. *Edison Experiments You Can Do*. New York: Harper & Row, 1960.

INDEX

c

Produced by
CommonPlace Publishing
2 Morse Court
New Canaan, Connecticut 06840

The text and display for this book have been typeset in various weights and sizes of Futura. A sans serif face designed in Germany in 1928 by Paul Renner, Futura has been widely copied and adapted for digital type systems. Based upon geometric shapes, the Futura letter is characterized by lines of uniform width. Previous typefaces reflected the irregularities of hand lettering.

We wish to express our gratitude to Joan A'Hearn of the Hall of Electrical History at the Schenectady Museum, Terry K. McGowan of the General Electric Lighting Institute, Douglas Tarr of the Edison National Historic Site, and Morgan Wesson and Jack Wenrich whose advice and research enriched this book. The index was prepared by Judith Kip.

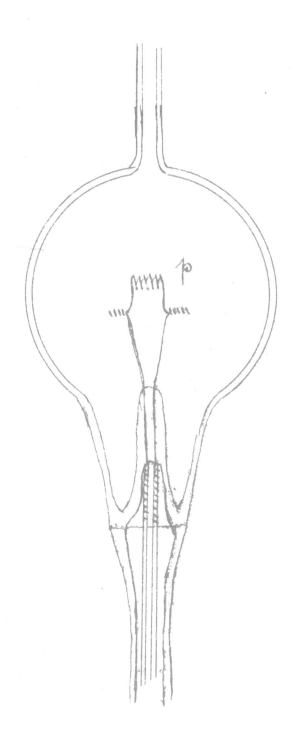